Paper Folding with Children

Translated by Anna Cardwell
Photography: Frechverlag and Lichtpunkt, Stuttgart
Step-by-step illustrations: Ursula Schwab

First published in German as *Das hab ich gefaltet*
by Frechverlag GmbH in 2013
First published in English by Floris Books in 2015

British Library CIP data available
ISBN 978-178250-174-9
Printed in China through Asia Pacific Offset Ltd

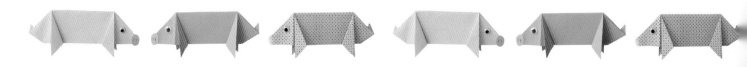

Paper Folding
with Children

Fun and Easy Origami Projects

Alice Hörnecke

Floris Books

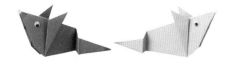

Contents

Before you begin

Types of paper

Origami paper is cut square with clean edges and is available in many colours and patterns. It is ideal for folding beautiful paper figures!

You can, however, use any type of paper as long as it is no thicker than normal writing paper (80 gsm), and does not make white creases when folded.

Special paper is advised for some figures. For example, waterproof paper will allow a folded boat to float without sinking. Tissue paper is also slightly transparent, which allows light to shine through beautifully.

Where A4 paper (21 x 29.5 cm or 8 ¼ x 11 ½ in) is not available, US standard letter size should produce similar results.

Tips and tricks

- Always fold your figures on a solid, dry base (a table is ideal).
- Beginners might want to start with larger paper: 20 x 20 cm (8 x 8 in). This makes it easier to perform tricky folds.
- When using brightly patterned paper it can be difficult to see the fold lines. Beginners may find one-sided, single-coloured origami paper better to start with, as the white underside makes it easier to tell which way round your figure is.
- Practice makes perfect! Folding can be quite tricky if you don't have much experience. If the figure you chose doesn't seem to work, put it aside for a while or try another figure first.
- The more exact your folds, the better the figures will look. Take your time and work carefully to achieve neat results.

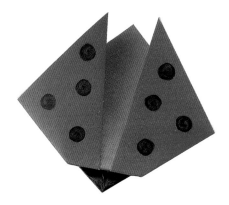

Folding tools

If you have several layers lying over each other and your fingernail is not strong enough, you may wish to use a folding tool such as a bone folder (made from plastic, not bone!) to help you make smooth, fine folds. The tip of the bone folder is also helpful when making sturdy corners.

Symbols

Valley fold: ▬ ▬ ▬ ▬ ▬

Mountain fold: ▬ • ▬ • ▬

Fold in the
direction of the arrow:

Turn the figure over:

Types of folds

Valley fold: fold the down in the middle as if you're closing a book.

Mountain fold: fold the edges of the paper in the opposite direction.

Inside reverse fold:
- Fold the corner down along the dashed line and unfold again to reveal a crease line.

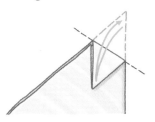

- Pull the paper layers apart slightly and push the corner in on itself along the crease lines.

Outside reverse fold:
- Fold the corner down along the dashed line and unfold.

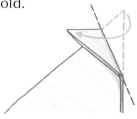

- Peel the corner back to turn it inside out – just like rolling up your sleeves.

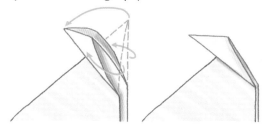

Ladybugs

Hiding in the bushes

You will need:

- Red origami paper, 15 x 15 cm (6 x 6 in)
- Black felt-tip pen

 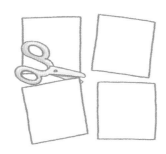

1. Fold and unfold the paper in half horizontally and vertically so that the creases form a cross. Cut along the lines to make four small squares: each one will make a ladybug or ladybird.

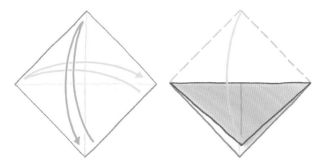

2. Place a small square down in front of you, red side down. Fold in half diagonally in one direction, then unfold. Now fold in half diagonally in the other direction to make a triangle, pointing downwards.

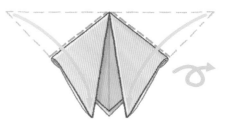

3. To make the wings, fold the left and right corners down almost to the centre line (leave a gap so there is a space between the wings!). Then turn the figure over.

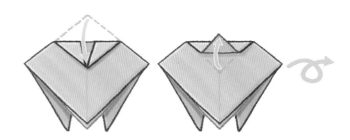

4. To make the ladybug's head, fold the top corner down to meet the centre. Next, fold it back upwards slightly so that the tip pokes out above the top line as shown.

5. Turn the ladybug over. Colour the head black and add dots to the wings using a felt-tip pen.

Tip

Repeat with the other three squares and you'll have a family of ladybugs ready to fly away home!

11

Ball and cup game

Can you catch the ball?

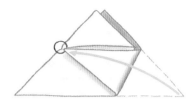

You will need:

- Colourfully patterned origami paper, 20 x 20 cm (8 x 8 in) or 15 x 15 cm (6 x 6 in)
- Wooden bead, diameter 1 cm (just under ½ inch)
- String or twine, 30–40 cm (12–16 in) long

1. Place the paper in front of you, patterned side down. Fold in half diagonally so that the triangle points upwards.

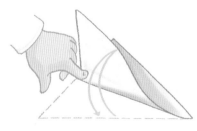

2. Make a small crease just over half way up the left side, but be careful not to fold along the entire length. This will be your marker point.

3. Fold the triangle's right point across to meet the marked point on the left.

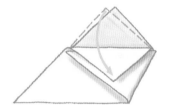 

4. Taking just the top layer, fold the top corner down and push into the pocket created by the previous fold. Turn the figure over and repeat steps 3 and 4 on the reverse.

5. To finish, open up the cup from the centre and punch a hole in a top corner. Tie the string through this hole and knot a bead to the other end. Can you catch the bead in the cup?

Tip

Once you are good at this game, improve your skill by using a smaller cup and a longer string!

Paper aeroplanes

Fly away!

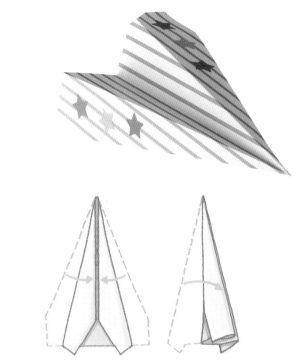

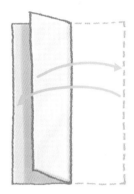

1. Place the paper in front of you, patterned side down. Fold in half lengthways and unfold again.

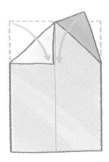 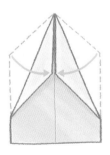

2. Fold both top corners down to meet the centre line. Then fold the new outer edges inwards in the same way.

3. Now fold the far outer edges inwards just as in step 2. Turn the plane over and valley fold it in half along your first crease.

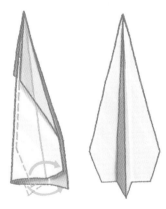

4. Crease all the folded edges firmly and then unfold the edges of the wings.

5. To finish, decorate your aeroplane with stars or other designs, and see how far it will fly!

Foxes

Crafty Mr Fox

You will need:

- Red, orange or brown origami paper, 15 x 15 cm (6 x 6 in)
- Black felt-tip pen

1. Place the paper in front of you, coloured side down. Fold in half diagonally to make a triangle pointing upwards.

2. Fold in half again to the left along the dashed line, then unfold.

3. Bring both side corners up to meet the centre line and flatten.

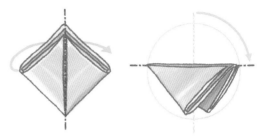

4. Mountain fold (away from you) along the centre line, as shown. Then rotate so that the triangle points downwards and the three loose edges are on the right.

5. Holding the bottom corner firmly, fold all three of the right edges left to meet the centre line.

6. Bend the top layer back to the right, then open out the middle layer and flatten downwards along the centre line to make the fox's head.

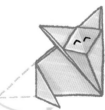

7. To finish, draw on some little eyes and fold the left corner in to make a tail.

Party hats ☆

Make them for your friends

You will need:

- Patterned paper, A4 (or US letter) or larger
- Glue

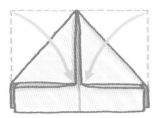

3. Fold both top corners inwards to meet the centre line to make a triangle top.

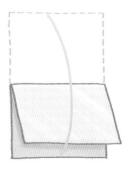

1. Valley fold the paper widthways in half.

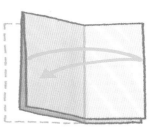

2. Fold in half widthways again, and unfold.

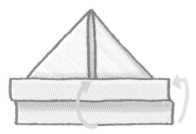

4. To make the brim of the hat, fold up the bottom edges over the front and back of the triangle.

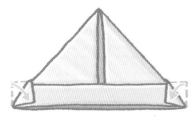

5. To hold everything together, fold the brim corners around the edge of the hat and glue in place.

Tip

The size of your hat depends on the size of paper used. To make large hats use newspaper or gift wrap.

Ducks ☆

Bobbing on a lake

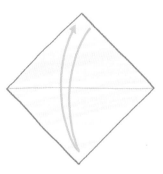

1. Place the paper coloured side down. Fold the paper in half diagonally and unfold again.

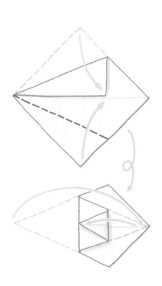

2. Fold the top and bottom corners inwards to meet along the centre line. This will form a sideways kite shape. Flip the figure over and fold the long left corner over to the right corner, then fold the point back on itself to the folded edge, as shown.

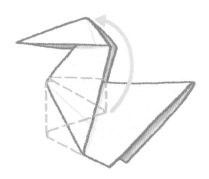

4. Holding the main body firmly below the tail, pull the neck upwards and flatten. Then pull the beak outwards to the left and flatten.

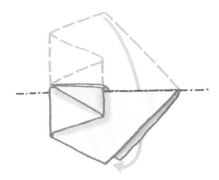

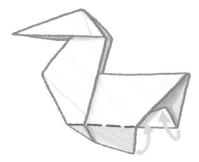

5. To make a standing base, fold both bottom corners inwards to meet each other.

3. Valley fold the figure in half lengthways along the original crease.

6. For some added detail, colour in the beak and glue on some googly eyes. Now it can swim away!

Pinwheels

Turning in the summer wind

You will need:

- Origami paper, double-sided colour,
  10 x 10 cm (4 x 4 in) or 15 x 15 cm (6 x 6 in)
- Push pin or map pin
- Wooden stick, 20 cm (8 in) long
- Double-sided sticky tape
- Hammer
- Scissors

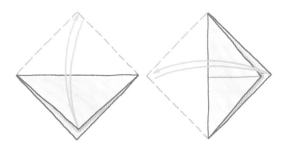

1. Fold and unfold the paper diagonally both ways.

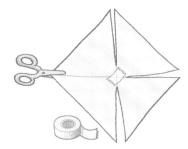

2. Attach a small piece of sticky tape to the centre point. Then cut a slit inwards along each crease line towards the sticky tape, stopping 1.5 cm (just over ½ in) from the centre point.

3. Without creasing the paper, loosely bend every second corner inwards and stick to the tape as shown.

4. To finish, ask an adult to help you press a drawing pin through the centre point and hammer it to the top of a stick.

5. Check that the pinwheel can turn freely – then it's ready to spin!

Tip

To make the pinwheel turn well, try creating a hole with a larger drawing pin and then using a thinner map pin to hold everything in place. The paper will spin more easily when slightly loose.

Paper monsters ☆

Chomp chomp

You will need:

- Yellow or orange origami paper, 15 x 15 cm (6 x 6 in)
- Scraps of red paper, black felt-tip pen, googly eyes, glue

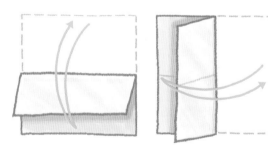

1. Place the paper with your desired colour or pattern face down. Fold and unfold the paper in half horizontally and vertically to make a cross.

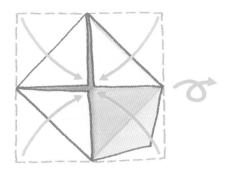

2. Now fold all four corners inwards to the centre point.

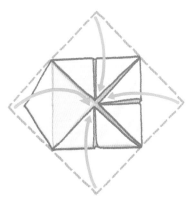

3. Turn the figure over and fold each corner to the centre point again.

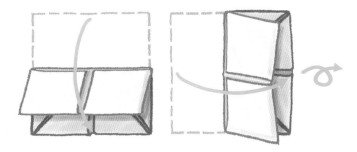

4. Fold and unfold the square in half horizontally and vertically to make new creases. Turn the figure over.

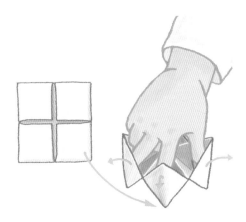

5. You will now see four flaps of paper pointing into the centre. Lifting the figure up, push your thumb, forefinger, middle finger and ring finger right into the corners of one square each, and squeeze them together. All four corners should fold in to meet at a point as shown.

6. You can now decorate your paper monster. Glue on googly eyes, cut out a red tongue and glue in place. Add any extra detail you can think of to make your monster unique!

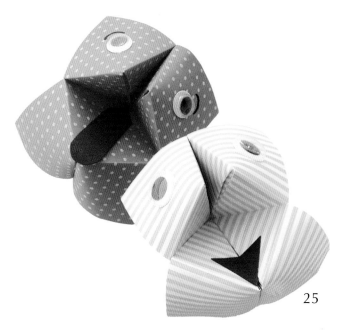

Love hearts

Show someone you care

You will need:

- Pink, red or patterned origami paper, 15 x 15 cm (6 x 6 in)
- Glue

4. Fold the left and right corners up again so that they now stick out above the fold. Turn the figure over.

1. Place the paper in front of you, patterned side down. Fold in half diagonally to make a triangle pointing upwards.

5. Fold the side corners inwards as shown.

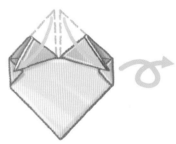

2. Fold the left and right corners up to meet at the top corner and unfold again.

6. To finish, fold the top corners down to the sides as shown and glue onto each folded corner. Turn the heart over and it is ready to give to somebody you love.

3. Fold the top corner down almost to the crease lines, leaving a 1 cm (just under ½ inch) gap.

Tip

Use these hearts for sending messages! Write or draw on the back of the heart before folding it.

Treasure boxes

For keeping little things safe

You will need:

- 2 pieces of patterned origami paper, 15 x 15 cm (6 x 6 in) or 20 x 20 cm (8 x 8 in)
- Scissors

1. First choose a pattern for the lid of the box and place the paper in front of you, patterned side down. Fold and unfold in half horizontally and vertically.

2. Fold all four corners inwards to meet the centre point.

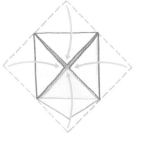

 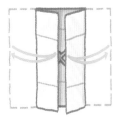

3. Now fold the top and bottom edges inwards to meet in the middle and unfold again. Do the same for the left and right edges.

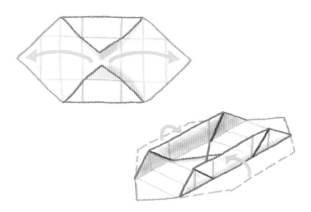

4. Unfold the left and right corners and turn the top and bottom edges up along the crease lines. This forms two sides of the lid.

5. To make the left side, lift up the left corner and make sure that the sides marked here with a red line fold inwards. Then, fold this upper-left corner down over the raised sides and along the bottom of the lid until it tucks neatly into the centre point. This will hold the left side firmly in place. Now repeat for the right side.

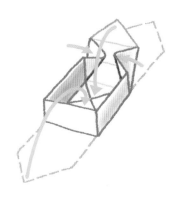

6. The lid is now complete. Next, choose a pattern for the container part of the box. This needs to be slightly smaller, so cut 5 mm (¼ in) off each edge of the origami paper, then follow the instructions for the lid. This box should fit snugly inside the lid!

Fish ⭐⭐

Happily swimming

You will need:

- Blue, preferably double-sided origami paper, 15 x 15 cm (6 x 6 or 10 x 10 in)
- Scissors
- Coloured scrap paper, googly eyes, glue, black felt-tip pen

1. Place the paper in front of you, coloured side down. Fold the paper in half diagonally, then unfold.

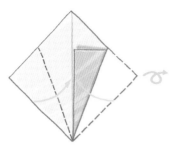

2. Fold the left and right corners from the bottom to meet the centre line, forming a kite shape. Turn the figure over.

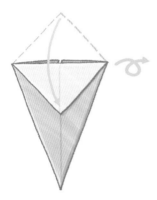

3. Now valley fold the top corner of your kite shape down and turn the figure over again.

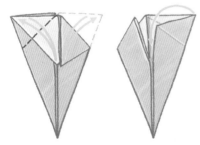

4. Fold both outer corners downwards along the centre line, and unfold again. Now press these corners inwards using the inside reverse fold (see page 8). This will leave two triangular flaps pointing upwards.

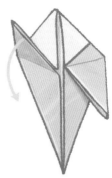

5. Fold these loose triangles downwards, as shown, to make fins.

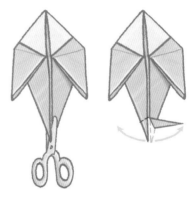

6. To make the tail, cut a slit roughly 1 cm (½ in) long along the centre line at the bottom. Then fan these corners outwards.

7. Now all you need to do is make a face for your fish. Glue on googly eyes and draw a mouth.

Tip

If you do not have double-sided colour paper or you want to make patterned fins, cut shapes out of scrap paper and glue them in place once the fish is complete.

Birds ☆☆

Singing in a tree

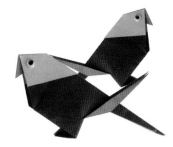

- Brightly coloured origami paper,
  15 x 15 cm (6 x 6 in)
- Googly eyes, glue
- Scissors

1. Follow steps 1 to 5 for the fish on pages 30–31.

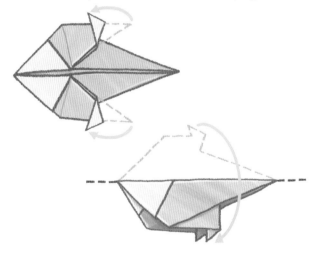

2. Fold the tips of the fins away from the main body to turn them into feet! Then turn the figure over and mountain fold in half along the spine (the feet should meet on the inside).

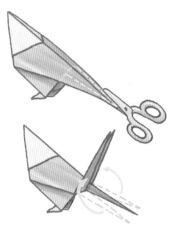

3. To make the tail feathers, cut a diagonal slit on each side of the centre line (the yellow dashed lines shown). Fold these outer strips upwards.

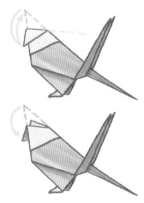

4. Fold the top corner of the head down diagonally as shown, leaving a small corner peeking out at the edge for a beak. Unfold and make an inside reverse fold (see page 8).

5. To finish, glue on some googly eyes and place your exotic bird up high.

Tip

Use patterned paper to make a bird with interesting feathers. Try it out!

Boats ☆☆

On the high seas

You will need:

- Waterproof, patterned A4 paper
  (or US letter)

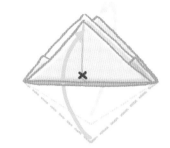

1. Make a party hat as described on page 19.

3. Fold the bottom corners up to the top on either side to make a triangle, then open up and flatten again as in step 2.

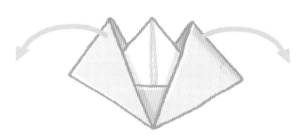

2. Hold the hat at the centre lines, open it up and flatten to make a square (the original corners will now lie over each other).

4. To finish, pull the top two layers apart a little and your boat will take shape.

Tip

To make the boat stand and float better, flatten it, push your thumbs into the hole in the bottom and loosen slightly. This will help to broaden the shape of the boat.

Cats ⭐⭐

Purring proudly

1. The cat is made out of two parts: a head and a body. We'll start with the body.

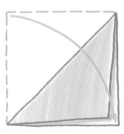

2. Place the paper in front of you, coloured side down. Fold in half diagonally so that it forms a triangle pointing bottom-right as shown.

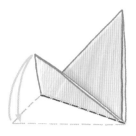
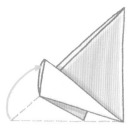

3. To make the tail, bring the bottom left corner about a quarter of the way up the triangle and fold along the dashed line, then unfold. Make an outside reverse fold along the creases (see outside reverse fold, page 8). This completes the body, which should be able to stand on its own.

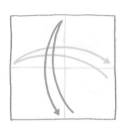

4. To make the head, place the paper coloured side down. Make four creases by folding and unfolding the paper in half horizontally, vertically and diagonally. The lines should all cross in the middle.

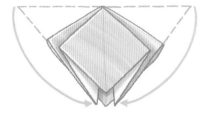

5. Now fold the paper in half diagonally so your figure forms a triangle pointing downwards. Push the right and left corners inwards along the creases using the inside reverse fold (page 8).

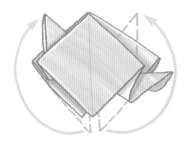

6. To make the ears, pull the bottom of the inside corners upwards so that they poke out above the head. Flatten them.

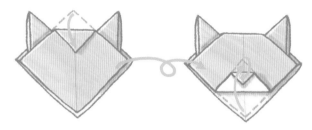

7. Fold the top corner between the ears away from you. Next, to give the face some detail, fold the top layer of the bottom corner upwards to the centre of the head. Then fold the tip back down again to make the nose. Fold the remaining bottom layer up inside the head to hold everything in place.

8. Push the head onto the top of the body and glue in place.

9. To finish your cat, draw whiskers and a striped coat, then add googly eyes!

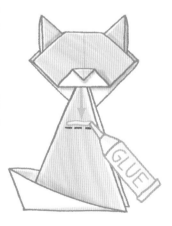

Spring surprises

To hide in your treasure box

1. First, fold a treasure box using the instructions on pages 28–29.

2. To make the spring, you will need two long, thin strips of paper. For a box made from 15 x 15 cm (6 x 6 in) origami paper, cut two 30 x 2 cm (12 x ¾ in) strips of paper; for a box made from 10 x 10 cm (4 x 4 in) origami paper, cut two 15 x 1.5 cm (6 x ²/₃ in) strips.

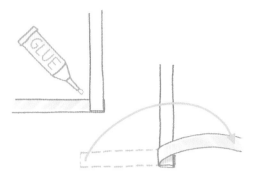

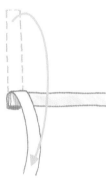

3. As shown in the image, make a right angle with the strips and glue their overlapping bases together. Then, fold the strips snugly one over the other, alternating until you reach the ends.

4. Trim off any excess material at the top if necessary, and glue together as shown.

5. Fold up a corner from the top layer and glue star or flower shapes to each side for decoration.

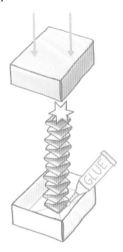

6. To finish, glue the bottom of the spring into the box and put the lid on. When you open the lid, it will jump out!

Tip

You can glue several springs into a single box. Cut the strips thinner so they all fit inside, and make them different lengths for fun!

Flower gifts ☆☆

To give away

1. Fold the paper in half vertically and cut along the centre crease. You will only need one half for a flower.

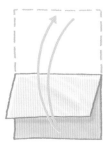

2. With the coloured side facing downwards, fold in half widthways and unfold.

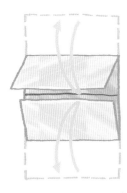

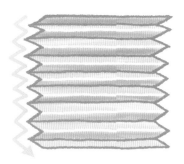

3. Fold the top and bottom edges in to meet the centre line. Unfold again. You will now have four horizontal sections (three creases).

6. When all the folds are completed, push them together along the crease lines so they fold back and forth like an accordion.

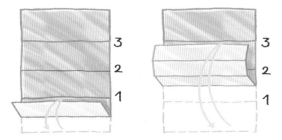

4. Each section will then need to be halved. To do this, fold the bottom edge to meet the first crease line, crease well and unfold. Then fold to the next crease line over the centre, and unfold. Repeat this process with the top edge.

5. Halve these narrower sections again. Turn the paper over and fold the bottom edge to the first crease line as before, then to every second crease. Then repeat the process from the other end until there are sixteen horizontal sections.

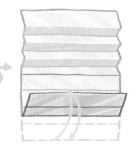

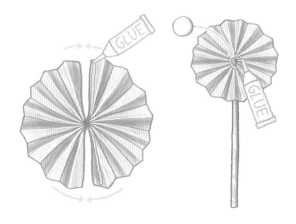

7. Now wind a piece of string around the centre and fan out the folds at the edge until they meet on each side. Then glue these sides together to make a complete circle. To finish, add a decorative centre to the flower and glue the back onto a stick to make the stalk.

Mice ☆☆

Squeak squeak

You will need:

- Grey origami paper, 15 x 15 cm (6 x 6 in)
- Pink and white scrap paper
- Googly eyes, glue
- Black pencil

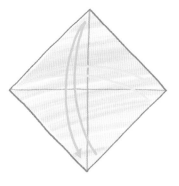

1. Fold and unfold the paper diagonally both ways.

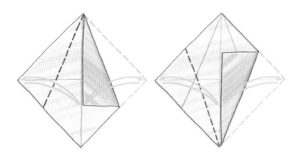

2. Fold the two top edges inwards to meet the centre line (like an upside down kite) and unfold again. Repeat from the bottom and unfold.

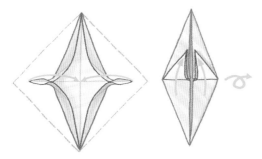

3. Squeeze the left and right corners together and push them into the centre to form a flat diamond shape with two triangles pointing out from the centre. Flatten these triangles upwards against the diamond.

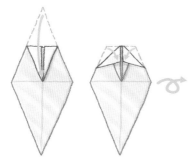

4. Turn the figure over and fold the top point inwards to meet the centre. Then fold the top left and right corners inwards again to the vertical centre line as shown.

5. Turn the figure over once more and fold the top flaps down to meet the centre horizontal line, one over the other as shown.

6. Mountain fold the paper in half along the red line to create the body of the mouse.

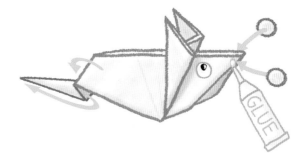

7. Finally, zigzag the tail as shown. Then glue googly eyes, cut out a pink circle for a nose and draw on whiskers with a black pencil.

Magic purse

For performing tricks!

....

You will need:

- White copy paper or designer paper, A4 (or US letter)
- Scrap paper for star shapes
- Glue

....

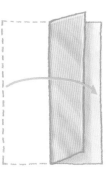

1. Place the paper in front of you, patterned side down. Fold in half lengthways so that the left side comes over to meet the right side.

2. Fold the top left corner to meet the right edge, forming a triangle. Then fold this triangle downwards as shown to create the main shape of the purse.

3. Fold the purse again to the left edge, making sure your fold is exact to avoid any paper sticking out later. You may find it helpful to use a bone folder to smooth all the layers down.

4. Now fold the bottom right corner up to meet the edge of your triangle.

5. Fold the remaining lower flap of paper away from you (behind the purse), and back again as shown.

6. Push this lower flap inside the centre of the purse to hold it all together.

7. Decorate your completed purse with stars, and make sure both sides are decorated the same so that you can trick people.

Tip

Your magic paper purse has four pockets: one at the top and three at the side. Put different sized coins into the three side pockets and leave the single pocket free. When you rotate the purse, you can put a coin in one compartment and it will appear to change its size when you bring another out from a different compartment. Practise in front of a mirror first to perfect your skill!

Flower displays ☆☆

Brighten up your window

1. You will need a 5 x 3 cm (2 x 1¼ in) rectangle for each leaf or flower petal (the flowers pictured use three or four petals).

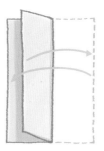

2. Fold and unfold each rectangle in half lengthways.

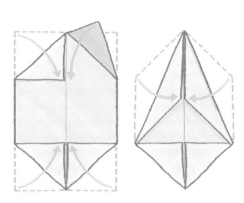

3. Fold all four corners inwards to meet the centre line. If you're making a leaf, fold the top corners in again to meet the centre lines – this completes the leaf!

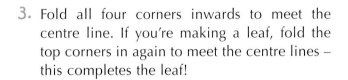

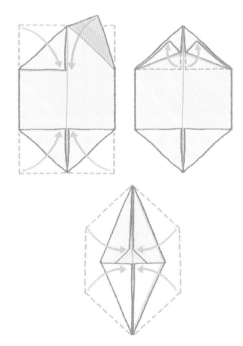

4. If you're making a petal, fold back the inner points of the top corners as shown. Now fold the top and bottom corners inwards to meet the centre line, creating a diamond shape.

5. Assemble the flowers in the following way: place each petal on top of the previous one, aligning the left side of the new petal with the centre line of the last one. Repeat with as many as you like and glue in place.

6. To make the stalk, cut a strip of paper 3 x 7 cm (1¼ x 2¾ in). Fold lengthways roughly 1 cm in (just under ½ in). Continue folding the strip over and over itself and glue the last fold in place to hold firm.

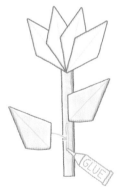

7. To finish, glue the flower and leaves to the stalk. The front should be the side without any visible folds.

Spaceships ☆☆

Shooting between the stars

You will need:

- Green or turquoise origami paper,
  15 x 15 cm (6 x 6 in)
- Silver or gold decorations, glue

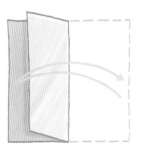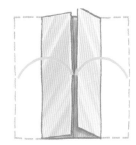

1. Fold the paper in half vertically, and unfold again. Then fold the left and right edges inwards to meet the centre line.

2. Mountain fold the top half away from you.

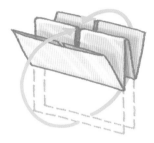

3. Fold up the two bottom edges to the front and back.

4. Next, tease the corners out from the inside left and right sides. Flatten to make four small triangles, two pointing out of each side.

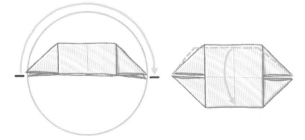

5. Rotate the figure 180° so the triangles slope downwards. Then unfold the top layer flat to reveal a square in the middle.

6. Now fold the top edge inwards (including the top segment of each triangle) to meet the centre crease.

7. Fold the entire bottom half back up along the centre crease, over the top of the figure.

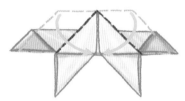

8. Next, fold the upper right and left edges diagonally down to meet the vertical centre.

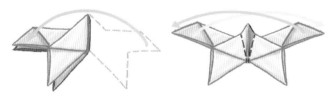

9. Valley fold the shuttle in half along the vertical line so that its wings lie over each other. Then, firmly holding the nose and base of the shuttle, fold the wings out on either side along the red lines as shown.

10. To finish, decorate your space shuttle with stars!

49

Frogs

Which will jump the furthest?

You will need:

- Green or green patterned origami paper, 15 x 15 cm (6 x 6 in)
- Googly eyes, glue
- Scissors

1. Fold the paper in half and cut along the crease to make two rectangles. You will only need one half for a frog.

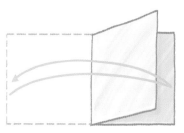

2. Coloured side down, fold the rectangle in half widthways and unfold again.

3. Fold and unfold each corner of the rectangle inwards to meet the centre line so that your rectangle has two sets of 'X' shaped creases.

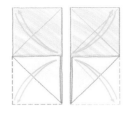

4. Now fold the top and bottom edges in to meet the centre line and unfold again.

5. Use the inside reverse fold technique (see page 8) on the left and right sides of each 'X' to form two flat triangles, one pointing up and one pointing down.

6. Fold the left and right corners of each triangle in to the centre.

7. Fold these corners back out to meet the folds you made in step 6. This makes the frog's feet.

8. Turn the figure over so it resembles a diagonal square with feet peeking out sideways from the top and bottom corners. Mountain fold and unfold to form a horizontal crease across the middle.

9. Fold the right and left corners downwards from the top to meet the centre crease line. This forms the shape of an upside-down kite on the frog's back.

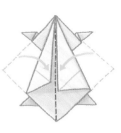

10. Fold the frog's bottom up and push the loose flaps of its back into the bottom pockets. Glue googly eyes to the head.

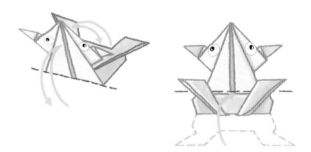

11. To make a jumping frog, fold the figure in half so that the feet lie over each other, and unfold. Then, fold the bottom half back on itself to the centre line you just created, and bend underneath the frog as shown. The frog will jump forward if you press down on the folded edge.

Bats ⭐⭐☆

Flying at night

You will need:

- Black and white or grey and white origami paper, 15 x 15 cm (6 x 6 in)
- Scissors
- Googly eyes or felt-tip pen

1. Place the paper in front of you, coloured side down. Fold diagonally downwards almost in half, leaving roughly 1–2 cm (¾ in) at the edge as shown.

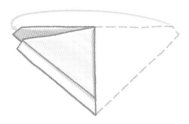

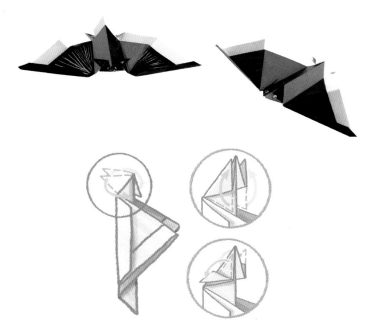

2. Mountain fold the right side underneath the left.

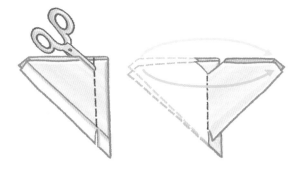

3. Cut two slits into the paper at the spots marked with a blue line: one diagonal slit roughly 2 cm (¾ in) at the top; and one vertical slit 1–2 cm (¾ in) up from the bottom. Then fold the wings back on each side along the dashed line.

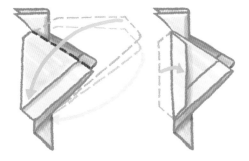

4. Now the wings are on the right, fold the top edges down to the left on each side so that they match the angle of the head. Then fold a thin strip back at the far left of the wings as shown.

5. To make the head, fold the two small triangles back on both sides towards the top of the wings. Then fold them back up again to meet the bat's nose, and bend back the tips of these triangles again to make little ears.

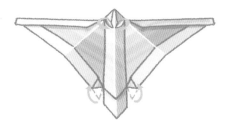

6. To finish, pull the wings apart and lift the ears up. Fold up the corners from the tail you cut earlier to make two pointed triangles. Draw eyes with a marker, or glue on some googly eyes.

Tip

Use magic scratch rainbow paper and you can draw a great pattern on the bat's wings!

Pigs ⭐⭐☆

Oink oink!

You will need:

- Pink origami paper, 15 x 15 cm (6 x 6 in)
- Googly eyes, glue
- If desired, scissors, scraps of pink paper and pink coloured pencil for detail

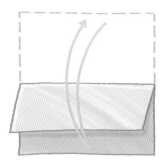

1. Place the paper coloured side down. Fold the paper in half horizontally, then unfold.

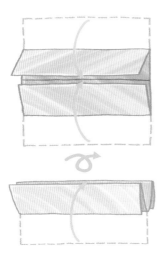

2. Fold the top and bottom edges inwards to meet the centre crease, then turn over. Fold the bottom half up along your original centre crease so that your figure forms an 'M' shape.

3. Fold the four top corners down along the dashed lines to meet the bottom edge, then unfold.

4. Now push all four corners inwards along their crease lines (see inside reverse fold, page 8).

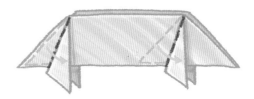

5. Fold all four corner flaps in towards the centre along the dashed lines. Then, unfold both of the corners on the left, keeping the ones on the right as they are.

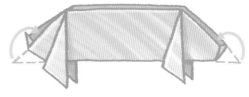

6. To make the legs, fold all four corner flaps down to meet the crease lines, as shown in the picture.

7. Using the inside reverse fold, push the corner at one end completely inwards to make a blunt snout. Do the same at the other end, but leave a pointy tip to make a tail. Alternately, simply bend the tail end to one side.

8. To finish, glue the eyes in place and draw or glue on a pig snout.

Toadstools ⭐⭐☆

In the undergrowth

You will need:

- Red and white origami paper, 15 x 15 cm (6 x 6 in)
- White scrap paper circles, glue

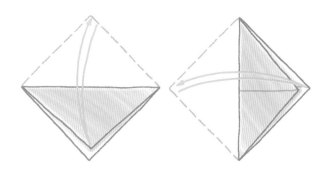

1. Place the paper in front of you, red side down. Fold and unfold diagonally in both directions to make an 'X'.

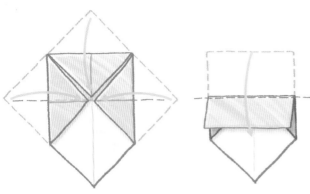

2. Fold three of the corners inwards to the centre, leaving the bottom corner untouched. Then fold the top half of the square down along the centre crease.

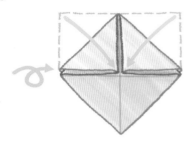

3. Turn the paper over and fold both top corners into the centre. Now the figure will be square again.

4. The next part is a little tricky: first pull out the paper from inside the top triangles, then fold inwards so that the corners meet at the centre. Don't worry if it doesn't look perfect – this is the back of the toadstool!

5. Now fold the top and bottom corners of the figure down and up as shown.

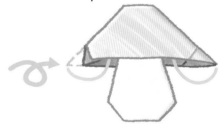

6. Turn the toadstool over and use an inside reverse fold (see page 8) at the left and right corners to round off the edges.

7. To finish, glue white paper circles to the top – and your toadstool is complete.

Dice ⭐⭐☆

Play a game!

You will need:

- 2 pieces of origami paper, 15 x 15 cm (6 x 6 in)
- For dots use coloured paper circles and glue, or a felt-tip pen, or stickers

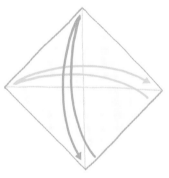

1. Place the first paper in front of you, coloured side down. Fold and unfold diagonally both ways.

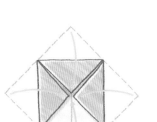
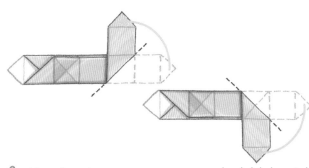

2. Fold all four corners into the centre point.

3. Divide each side into thirds by marking two equidistant spots 3.5 cm (just under 1 ½ in) apart on each of the four edges. Fold the top and bottom edges inwards at the marked points and unfold again.

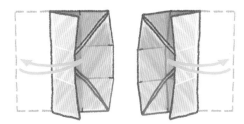

4. Repeat this process with the left and right sides.

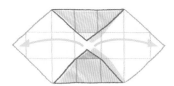
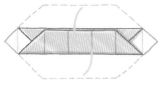

5. Unfold the left and right triangles, then fold the top third down and the bottom third up to lie over one another.

6. Keeping the centre square steady, fold the right half of the figure upwards at a right angle, then downwards at a right angle along the diagonal dotted lines. This will make the shape of an 'X' on the second square from the right. Repeat this process with the left half of the figure.

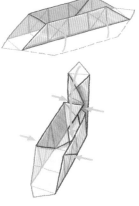

7. Keeping the central square firmly on the table, unfold the top and bottom thirds so they stand upright. Then fold the left and right edges upwards and inwards to form a box. (You may want to revisit step 5 of the instructions for the treasure box on pages 28–29.)

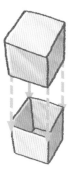

8. One side of your die will be missing. To complete its other half, repeat steps 1 to 7 using another piece of paper which has been trimmed 5 mm (¼ in) smaller on each side. When it is complete, push it inside your first box and your die is complete.

9. To finish, draw or glue dots in place and your game can begin!

Butterflies ⭐⭐☆

In beautiful colours

- -

You will need:

- Coloured and patterned origami paper, 15 x 15 cm (6 x 6 in)

- -

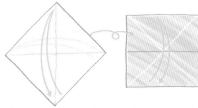

1. Place the paper in front of you, coloured side down. Fold and unfold diagonally both ways. Then turn the paper over and fold it in half horizontally.

2. Use an inside reverse fold (page 8) to push the edges inwards along the dashed lines as shown. The coloured side of the paper should be on the outside.

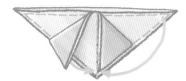

3. Lie the triangle flat, pointing downwards. Taking only the top layer, fold the right and left corners down to meet the centre line.

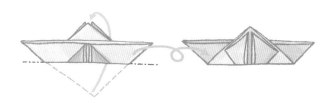

4. Fold the bottom of the whole figure back under itself along the dashed dotted line until it pokes out the top from behind. Now turn the figure over.

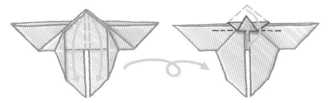

5. The next step is a little tricky. Fold the top layers of both inner triangles downwards as shown. This will pull the sides upwards at the right and left. Flatten these sides and crease them well.

6. To make the head, turn the figure over, then fold the top corner downwards and back up again as shown.

7. Fold the butterfly in half from tip to tail. Then fold the wings back up along the diagonal dashed line of the body. Unfold the body a little and your butterfly is complete!

61

Resources

AUSTRALIA
Morning Star
www.morningstarcrafts.com.au

NORTH AMERICA
The Waldorf Early Childhood Association of North
America maintains an online list of suppliers at:
www.waldorfearlychildhood.org

UK
Myriad Natural Toys
www.myriadonline.co.uk

Waldorf Schools

In 2015 there were over 1,000 Waldorf schools
and 1,500 kindergartens in over 60 countries
around the world. Up-to-date information can be
found on any of the websites below.

AUSTRALIA
Association of Rudolf Steiner Schools in Australia
www.steineroz.com

NEW ZEALAND
Federation of Rudolf Steiner Schools
www.rudolfsteinerfederation.org.nz

NORTH AMERICA
Association of Waldorf Schools of North America
www.whywaldorfworks.org

SOUTH AFRICA
Southern African Federation of Waldorf Schools
www.waldorf.org.za

UK
Steiner Waldorf Schools Fellowship
www.steinerwaldorf.org.uk

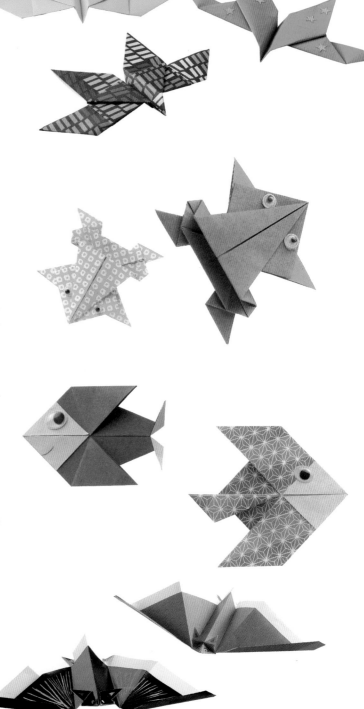

Weaving With Children

Ute Fischer

Papercraft

Angelika Wolk-Gerche

Making Soft Toys

Karin Neuschütz

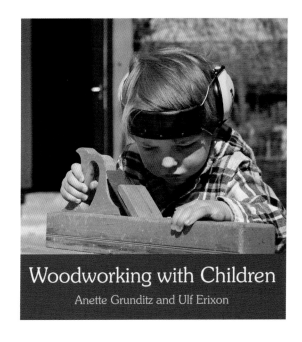

Woodworking with Children

Anette Grunditz and Ulf Erixon

Finger Strings

A Book of Cat's-Cradles and String Figures

Magic Wool Fruit Children

Crafts Through the Year

Thomas and Petra Berger

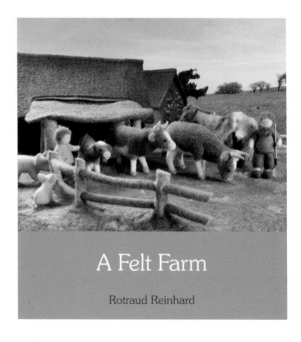

A Felt Farm

Rotraud Reinhard